Ay

Ay

Poems

Joan Houlihan

[signature: Joan Houlihan]

T|P

Tupelo Press
North Adams, Massachusetts

Library of Congress Cataloging-in-Publication Data
Houlihan, Joan, 1951–
[Poems. Selections]
Ay : Poems / Joan Houlihan. -- First edition.
     pages cm
ISBN 978-1-936797-41-7 (paperback original : alk. paper)
I. Title.
PS3608.O85545A6 2014
811'.6--dc23

                              2013034398

First edition: February 2014.

Cover and text designed by Rose Carlson.
Cover photograph: Jeffrey Levine. Used courtesy of the artist.

Tupelo Press
P.O. Box 1767
243 Union Street, Eclipse Mill, Loft 305
North Adams, Massachusetts 01247
Telephone: (413) 664–9611 / Fax: (413) 664–9711
editor@tupelopress.org / www.tupelopress.org

Tupelo Press is an award-winning independent literary press that
publishes fine fiction, nonfiction, and poetry in books that are a joy
to hold as well as read. Tupelo Press is a registered 501(c)3 nonprofit
organization, and we rely on public support to carry out our mission
of publishing extraordinary work that may be outside the realm of
large commercial publishers. Financial donations are welcome and
are tax deductible.

For their strength and brilliance and love:
Alex and Ian and, as always, Eric.

CONTENTS

III. *Wherein Ay confronts his grief.*

IV. *Wherein greb confronts his guilt.*

V. *Wherein greb & Ay journey together.*

KITH & KIN

us	group of people who speak as one
father	leader of the us; father of Ay, brae, & greb
mother	also called g'wen; late wife of father; mother of Ay, brae, & greb
Ay	eldest son, who separates from the us
brae	youngest brother & caretaker of Ay
greb	middle brother & attacker of Ay
thems	enemy of the us, who once held Ay captive

I

Wherein Ay recovers his speech & mobility & is treated as a god.

WHO KILLS the past
knows it is buried
in the same air Ay breathe.
Only a hair is needed to keep you, mother.
Only a bit of bone.
Comfort, comfort, Ay am my own.

Wanting simple, a sun like water, a flow and stir of air.
Warm stone, black-warm, dirt scent and bird.
Ay am put out to weather.

Animal eyed me here—heaving, breathing over—
felt by smell for me and loomed,
sifted my hair as it neared and sniffed
then left. Comfort, comfort me.

A thresh of sticks and vine, hand-carried
high—Ay am my own weight carried by,
kind horse, kind mother, gone.

Wherein Ay recovers his speech …

NOT AS ONE who knows the ground
but woken to a standing,
Ay rose and held as bird would hold
for want of weather, flight.
Far, the hard light grew.
The us were down in sleep.
Fire blacked away.
None would know me
colding there. Ay stood and stept
as calf that has no mother-side,
as a weak thing made, then fell
and lay in a smaller place to wait.
Where a noise had been
Ay let a quiet in.

AS LIGHT DOES to a ground at rise
high and quiet in its dark
spread low and warm on leaf and grass,
Ay come back slow, hand to leg
and rise to walk—

                              put one leg out

keep one behind

                              put one leg out

keep one behind

Stirred to wake, the us come out
to huddle round.
Ours shadow wore a shape
of many bodies going toward,
going back, hunched and swayed,
legs at odds and walking strange.
There were no way to go but as the whole.

SHOULDER-HEFTED, left unsteady,
leaned as in a wind, not strong.
Still felt the rock that knocked me shut.
Slow-blown through, an ear,
Ay hear deep quiet in the air, an after-clap
poured out, as thunder spent. Done by night,
a wax burnt down, Ay waited,
wasted. Rain washed hush across the field.
Long-sealed Ay could not speak.
But talk ran on, a river in me
and made a quiver, quick,
that Ay would touch my tongue to it,
break the sudden run of it, stop
the rush and hum of it,
that, deep-held, kept me silent as a god.

SUMMER RIPE in the ground, deer fled
red-gold in the wood. Sticks put sharp
in the side bled the trail.

For antlers the us downed the dying
and broke from the heads of the kneeling.

Gripping antler and stick,
day-long they would build
what must be built by digging down.

As day burnt low the tinder piles were tossed.
Hemp stalk held above, one took from a tall
and torched them all to rising. In the wood, a deer,
head bowed, showed its blood spots brightening.

DUG IN THE SUN and the sun burnt them sick—
chalk and flint and hard—
and the us built a hole for ours dead to climb down
and nest at the bottom in bones.

Bend, rise, bend, rise—clack
the rubble high, and the beds
were black, deep and long
for all ours dead to lie down.

As small fires crawled the hill,
Ay watched the long darks walk.

UNKILLED AND COME, one
then many, out from woods,
at the edge and known—
all the red horses spy.

One would find me
with lowered head, halt
hims walking toward, an offer
in hims bare-gleamed back,
neck thrust, muscled for the strap
and long with a wish to be captured.

Helper! Friend! Bearer of us!
Eye-mild, kin to, and kind, you
are for work and under a heat
will pull at rock, make a strong
around ours father, gone.

TO BUILD AN ALTAR to ours father,
Ay am walked to where light hung.
Slow and slower over ground,
shadow-soaked, Ay would know
build it here! and stop.
Horse would come, strapt
to rock, and tug with force.
The us pry stone from stone,
raise a wall with cracks and watch
how father makes a shape of sun between.

STICKS BROKE SOFT, fell shorn
of green. The smell—damp rot.
Face-hid, the dead stoop
to fires that cannot light
and rub thems hands in air.

As rains come sharp, not spared,
all are still and bent
lit by bolt and held.
What lives outside must come in—
Father, come in from the rain-night.
Father, come in from the cold.
Come in and rub yours hands.

MORNING, BORN, kept
limb to limb, a fruit new-grown
to where it riped before. What felt had sound—
bird and sheep—and known as son, Ay am walked
to the altar, propped to the mouth-hole to speak.

MORNING, FRESHER from a storm,
told a scent of dirt and moss.
Alone at the altar, Ay smelled the rain, its past.

One who hurt a horse were brought.
The us made a hurt for him.
Quiet, took the water called a burn
and put a smoke around hims head.

One were chilled with the death-cloth
pulled to hims chin.

And all this when Ay had no talk,
when field-bud, raked by wind,
splayed open, full of scent.

LIT LEAF, AND ONE cast shade
on another as day strove, rain-sunk.
Ours dead stood out against the sky
not knowing they had died.

New-kill, feathered and furred,
bowls of blood and milk, spilled drip-
downs of a she-goat far from hers warm.
Lifted, held high by the us,
Ay am put to the rock-hole to speak:
Go back to the dirt, go back.
And the dead heard this and went into the earth.

Then from braes hands some still-held buds
dropt onto altar-stone. He stood as a shook torch
burning to tell: *many were here, and gone.*

At evening, when ours most are lost,
Ay see them stand along the hill,
gathered and alike.

UNDER THE BODE of sky
old-eyed horses stood.
Some come to the altar
hobbled and bent.
One with a long foot
dragging. One with eye unshut.
Ailing or struck, each knelt to be lower.
Ay lay in a quiet to let them.
Day burnt down a long want,
drank the moon pale.
Old moon, who knew me best.

AND A CLOTH BLED high on a stick
raised for the noise of new dark.
Fields were spelt and fire-
smoke, harvest turned animal, pelt-
stripped for meat, tree-mad with fruit
at the last. Winter ate into the us,
putting the lamb to pen
and Ay spoke as a fire low-burning:
All to be told again. All to be done.
The us pulled field of its grain.
Deer, rough-coated for winter fled,
hid from the us, went strange.
By sun winter-lit in the eye of a lamb
by a great tree in rags, aging,
wind-cut and high to sun,
the cloth soaked full, bled down.

EYED FROM A BRANCH as feather
brushed day into light and Ay
called again to the altar, rise.
Goat bled on the ground of ours dead,
staked, open-eyed, dripped down.
Then soft and led on a hemp-rope,
the padded lamb comes to stand.
Coat, hand-deep.
Eye, rolled white.
Ay touched the head bent down.
Let him. Let him go.

Wherein Ay recovers his speech …

THEN SHEEP WENT spared, berries clung, small to shade,
and where they stept a seed took root and flowered white.
If this were milk, then a lamb would come, bend to it, tender it,
take to hims mouth and be fed from it. Bowed and chewing,
eye to the hill, then in the fog curve a face toward us, in the fog
come soft.

SMOKE WILL FIND and flood the sky.
Whatever wants a fire
will warm. Goat, cow, horse—
all will be cared for as Ay, wrapt
as calf in mother-skin,
blink at birth as through a cloth
to see the shape of what were lost.
As seed would take from sky
what gives it light, Ay take from sun-
fed day what will not end
and is not mine again.

II

Wherein Ay leaves the us
& meets the dead.

AY LEFT THE US before dawn-dark
rose to its born and rising.
Bird let cry to the egg in hiding.
Ay found and cupped and fled with it
before cold could take the quick of it.

When the wind stopped Ay killed.
Bled in broad day, quick-stripped
bare, the boar, still whole, Ay tucked in cloth,
the deer, trunk-cut to the plenty and froze.

In loudening hoots against the dark,
Ay buried what had not burned yet
under the long snow falling
soft on the cut of living.

WHAT EATS GRASS slow and bent-
necked, eyed from the side, is deer.
Through branches hung with bee-nest,
swung, and the swarm
hums the air. At the edge,
one deer holds tall.

Ay want what is not *Ay*—
furred antler stript to a shine.
Flank. Hoof. Meat.
When the head turns, Ay stand,
aim the spear—to mine.

DANCED THE ANTLERS, knelt
hims body—large still beast
killed to make me alive.
Char-water, river-rock
stand the night.
As spark on spark fed
sky-cold stars,
smells bramble the fire.
Powders of hazel-shell flare.
Ay will be offered too.
Next world, will you have me?

HUNG AS SKINS some last leafs strove
not to twist, the oldened gone to yellow

first. Cold ran the field to frost. One light
crawled long grass, climbed the top.

Moon smeared sky, cloud
smoked sky to night.

MASSED HAIR and warm, arm bent,
Ay wake to sky part dawn and slow
as sun cracked through a cloud
and spread, drop-spotted red by red
along the hill where father led us once.
Tell me then, what was Ay doing there?
Furred and sly, a small mole
noses near.

COLD HEIGHT, SEED-soaked,
what lives toward shows the marks:
auk and owl, insect, horn,
leaf-borne or buried in dirt.
All the sun-soft sheep.
Things the night takes away.

Over the grove, freed of hive,
a bee lifts from its summer bed
to a slit of light one deep
telling its own stung way.
Small, and it lives toward the swarm,
rare from the cluster and blind.

Age, a parcel of rag, ay drag
under open sky.
As if ay lived that long
in cold and cave and chalk,
buried in light holes or soaked with night.
As if in the heat of birds.

Hand, one hand, and Ay tap my chest—
Here, where father built—
then pasture hims shadow, tend him,
coming from sleep as all things do
alive toward the first fires of day.

IN THE MOTHER WATERS of morning,
a flush of fish and leap
and ours dead put a talking on wind:

What burnt us off an isle
stung ours crops to frost,
took ours horse for meat,
bit him down to bare?

What kind of winter was burning?
What fit the wind to its grass?
What took ours walk and slow,
pulled us like smoke through air?

Be ours comfort and cover us.
Give us a bowl and place to drink.
Keep us, keep us warm.
Ours bed is a night and gone.

Then sky put down with a shiny stone
the knowing lodged in its head.

Wherein Ay leaves the us …

/26

SHUT BY DAY as shade in sun,
out by night and bundle-slung,
they stoop as fires strike up
and put the meat to cook. Hand to mouth
the same, but they eat only air.
Ay see them round a smoke as thin as mine
nested close and on the ground.
Cast from light, the dead are what they were
and rise to doing what they must.
Ay see them now, busy on the hill.

FROM HILLS ROCK-ruined and split with sun,
the dead come down with a woe:
Ours sail was wind and green. Ours boat,
a body of creak and rope.
Us turned to the wave and the wave
came up salt, the wave came up salt
and sudden. Us were bathed and wed to it,
brushed with the foam and scent of it,
ours body tight-sewn into it.
Many agains, us are tossed
in the endless sift of sea.

Wherein Ay leaves the us ...

THEN EASE, A LETDOWN of breeze,
calm to branch, born in air, rinsed
and faint as behind a cloth they come
in a dumb-show, crowded slow.
Bundle-backed, tethered in step,
hand to shoulder of one before.
Ay see mother coming kind,
empty swaddle in hers arms.
Father, slower, walks behind.

ONE SPEAKS through a hole.
Air whistles through.
In the mingle many louden—
Us were dirt. Ours crown a vine.
Roots of us knotted, knuckled and furred.
Under the earth ours eyes still looked.
Plow stroked ours bed and us woke.
Then one came forth, strong in shape,
whitened from death, hair to the waist,
hand upraised to be held. *Mother!*
Ay felt hers cold pass by.

THEN SHE HAD A DEATH in me, knees drawn up
and my bowl and cloth rinsed through with her.
As morning takes night, field closes the hare
and Ay am folded into her.

Over my head, catalpas rattle,
shadow and bother the branch.
Is this hers white? Dress me.
Hers rain? Wash me with that.
Hers bowl? Feed me to empty.
Hers colding? Ay am forgot.

Then mask me the g'wen, hers skin
being mine, and body that pools
in the brine of her, rivers the silt and stone of her
wrapt in the warm of hers fell.
She were the watcher and tender of pyres
when the wet grass shined with quiet
and Ay lean to the mouth-hole: *Ay, mother.*

THEN AY KNOW my horse,
let alive and out of days,
hide now paled, hind leg slow
to drag, lower head to lift,
hoof-split, burred and rough from the dirt.
Strange when Ay speak to him.
Tremble runs under him.
What owned him fills him.
Same horse Ay tamed are you the same?
Mane-tangled, lank, and under brow,
hims eye as from a coal half-burnt
sparked up. Ay pulled my body on—
start, rear, run—
and did not loose but stormed and shaken
held as leaf to stem. Sky could hear
the finding cry Ay made.

THEN MASK ME HORSE: storm, strap and mane,
redden me, berry and clay. Lead me,
tame, Ay am hims sound: warm
muscle, sun to hims running—
breath-born, neck-stretched, blowing.

Kept on and a field scraped open (crack of rock
on the plow) kept on and a higher cry after
(hit by rock, struck down).

Dawn soaked the sky—
Who hurt me?
Then shone to me
wood-deep, a torch-light
moving between the trees.

III

Wherein Ay confronts his grief.

A CRUSH of oily plant and treated white, wrapt and reached
by root, sky-touched and still, a bud in leaf. Make of me a body.
Hand and foot, bind me tight, scented green: this is my dressing,
done. Ay lived and spoke to what Ay was. No matter if you hear.
Across my forehead fingers sweep a clay. Remember what Ay was
and am. Kind horse, lie down beside.

GLAD OF THE WIND. It keeps the hungry
away, puts a noise over the sky not to hear
what would come close at night.
Horse shadows the ground,
squeak of grass-chew, flank
shivers and the side-eye sees me.

THE LONG-EARED, the white
and the brown come. Bird less hurt by light
than dark, each part of each
locked by frost, tips of beaks chipped
on branches of salt.
Damage of sand on the feed,
mouse-kill in a small skull, a vole uneaten—
sky covered all of it in grit, and blind
from shoulder to pit to eye
Ay am hollow and lit by a hunger.

IN LIGHTS WANDER and more
to watch for and run from; handful
of hair, bristle or brim of fat and boil,
only my sack, nosed by horse, supped down
to little grain, and a hare once stamped
to breaking, hard meat. These gristles tell.
These jointed pieces tell. These mouth noises
tell. In the scant light of old moon
Ay think of him who once was us.

GROUND AY FELT Ay stood on
my horse my sweat and sway Ay leaned on
buzz and feed of sun Ay held to
mounting light, the ground Ay felt
every day one day
body no longer the body
Ay lived in like a hut.
When it reaches me the sun will be cold.

WHERE WATER RIBS sand
and filches root,
shells strike and rub,
shatter-crack. Dry had wet
but there is no grass,
no plant holds down and blooms.
Rock stays, there bone,
deep-printed in sand as the body
holds what struck or moved it
pressed in a dry bed.

SUN TO THE EYE and bark
thick where once stripped,
plant crowds plant
and the deepest root freshens.
This way Ay went
daylong toward, nightlong
with a sense of where,
walking the bones of the leg,
the flesh of the foot
as the full moon passes
into its dark and returns brighter.
Arm to elbow Ay lean toward the fire.
What begins and ends in smoke,
flicks and licks to sky.
All will be night in the part not seen.
Smoked moon, a rim, a ring.
Where he is, is far.

Wherein Ay confronts his grief.

HOW DEEPLY HID depends on the hurt.
Head down, toward dirt,
as if Ay will find him there, as if
spread among rock and rock, he lives
in what once kept him out, the body he was,
the voice he was, and what Ay am
and want no more of. Ay long to return
to where father returned. Torch-tip of last sun
snuffed and what seeded in me, stunts.
Unkeep the horse from hims halter,
unwrap the cloth from my body.
As the weight of every living thing roots in
Ay long for him who has kept me
away in the back of hims dark.

QUICK IN THE CAIRN what bird had once:
a neck kept straight by spine,
ribs still bound to a chest.
A beast, complete.
What raised and moved him
unjoins from muscle
and twines like a hemp unused.
As if the sun had rubbed him long
then put him out in a hole full of rain.

THEN MASK ME prey for what could die:
ox and cut and deer stuck long
to bleed a morning on the hill.
Kept on and found a cornered boar
and all hims cry. Kept on and found
the place inside an owl. Kept on
and found the sheep, throat-cut—
who did this?—
Ay fell still to hear. Then sounded through
fingerbone, given by pyre,
bent black and burnt: *Greb.*

IV

Wherein greb confronts his guilt.

TREE-DARK, STRAYED far,
half-sunk in snow, unslept.
Face taken by winter, tight.
Greb never speaks. From the ashpit,
an ember, loaded with light.
From cold, a cold life grows.

MANY TIMES bound to shadow,
greb goes with stick, goes on stone,
to find what shines, what makes it shine,
a haven from pain—from brother!—
mother-stained and favored.
Greb struck with a rock
to see Ay feel, to see
Ay fail and fall.
Now dread walks him
and mouth makes him say it—
Him fell!
From what?
A boar.
And on grebs fearing comes the moon
up on a crown of fir.
You did it. Rain said that.

TALL SKY shoulders night,
comes from down and from dale.
Fretted from fire, comes in a blaze.
Greb smells dawn-grass and grain
sowed green. Hears the wood-brimmed sticks.
What crackles through leaf-open trees?
What stands before greb wanting touch?
Greb felt hims finger into its wound:
This is what you made, it said.

SNOW-TRACKS blown over, unshown.
What stayed were flint in hims hand.
He washed with snow-water, dried
with sun, takes after a fur that goes into a hole,
skins for the warm of him, meat for the lasting.
The wood-cracked camp blacks snow.
Harder than this is the knowing that shone
through him, into hims bones.

WHAT WANTS GREB living
has a watch on him,
knocks to the tree, around the trunk
takes to branch, a bird, an eye—
something wants him alive.
Who bore him? g'wen.
Who brothered him? Ay.
Ay, the elder, favored.
Greb fisted from that,
made pain hims say.
Now sparrow-sprung in a dark-led wood,
in fear a beast would split hims scalp
or mark with tooth who slept there,
greb startles to hear:
Struck and fallen, by your hand.
Risen and put to show.
A godly pelt, a man wrapt in,
hair on one side, blood the other—
your brother wanders, never whole.
That which was the world is gone
seasoned by hims dawns.

Wherein greb confronts his guilt.

/52

V

Wherein greb & Ay journey together.

NOT ALL STRONG, one side slow, my foot
not true and each step Ay remember
who made me so. Bird loft. Wind talk.
Ay stop and something stops
one crackle-step behind.
Greb!
And he comes soft-faced, eyes down,
open-palmed. A little away
we stand and watch each other hard
and do not stir
as leaf would stir, branch crack.
Bird flapped quick.
That wound is mine.
Greb spoke and neared.
Ay bent my head to show it,
took hims touch.
We stood the quiet together:
the forest, the bee-rubbed air.

Wherein greb & Ay journey together.

HURT IS COMFORT, fed.
And now who hurt me, feeds me.
Meat. And it chars on the fire. Meat.
And it juices the mouth.
Who held me captive to a wound,
who let the dark rain down, comes by now
to tend the pain he owns.

DAY ON DAY falls
and falls. Night comes, a hill of ocean.
Dawn, a sea-stained sail.
And we walk and hunt as before,
ours old wood crowded small
with leafy shade, breaking bud,
crawled with ant and worm,
bee- and moth-lit, rabbit- and fox-swept,
deer foot marking the trail.

Wherein greb & Ay journey together.

ROUGH-BACKED in dawn
and jagged, cloud-mad with insect
and light, the blackened town juts up.
Silent on a hill above, we stop.
This town, this ruin, Ay were captive here,
left it burning when water went foul,
when sick beasts staggered to eyes rolled white,
when bodies, sick, were piled and lit.
My head were as torch, my body wax.
Greb went down the hill first.

RAG SMELL. FIRE smell.
Bed blacked. Bowl.
The quiet come from living done.
Shadow built the walls, holed and cribbed with light.
Vine felt cracks and fingered in.
Were sky inside
and what the wind-holes left, a wind.
We walk the last. What were floor
hove rock and root.
Flame-eaten walls in rubs of wood,
scraps the burn left licked
now licked with dirt.

Wherein greb & Ay journey together.

OUT BACK, UNPLOWED, a ragged row
of not-grown fruit, the rest in husk or ash
and in the low empty
where once thems bodies lay out lit
and sick, a soil of powder and splinter,
matter that stays for the sun.
Not for us, a boar under ash.
Greb pokes hims stick straight through
to see the crawlings go.

STRICKEN WITH SLEEP we lay
by tindered huts, roof-bared
pens where the sick sheep burned first.
Waked by the scent of brine and the salt-call of the sea,
all day we follow the eye of it moving between the trees,
looking for trails to it, hearing the lash of it,
not to hunt but to follow
the voices that called us down.

AND A RAIN let down from sky
and a salt rain came off the sea, and wave
and wave lashed higher, milk and green.
In the rush of water stood ours dead:
In what wave breaks ours kin, hove over the side and left?
Sorrow the eye does not forget.
Past has ashed ours heads with it.
Rain and wave will wash us in
what eats sky slow, the sea.
And on us too, the same rain fell,
unsparing, and everywhere quenched.

Acknowledgments

Thanks to the editors of the following publications, where some of these poems appeared, in certain cases with different titles and in earlier versions.

Academy of American Poets, website www.poets.org/:
"RAG SMELL. FIRE smell."

Boston Review: "COLD HEIGHT, SEED-soaked", "NOT AS ONE who knows", and "SHOULDER-HEFTED, left unsteady"

Harvard Divinity Bulletin: "AND A CLOTH BLED high"

Indiana Review: "DANCED THE ANTLERS, knelt" and "THEN EASE, A LETDOWN of breeze" (as "Mine ease a letdown")

Poetry: "A CRUSH of oily plant", "THEN SHE HAD A DEATH in me", and "WHO KILLS the past" (as "Who kills my history")

Southampton Review: "AS LIGHT DOES to a ground at rise", "AY LEFT THE US before dawn-dark", "HUNG AS SKINS some last leafs strove", and "TO BUILD AN ALTAR to ours father" (as "To find the father")

Taos Journal of Poetry and Art: "DUG IN THE SUN and the sun burnt" and "LIT LEAF, AND ONE cast shade"

OTHER BOOKS FROM TUPELO PRESS

Fasting for Ramadan: Notes from a Spiritual Practice (memoir), Kazim Ali
This Lamentable City (poems), Polina Barskova,
    edited and introduced by Ilya Kaminsky
Circle's Apprentice (poems), Dan Beachy-Quick
The Vital System (poems), CM Burroughs
Stone Lyre: Poems of René Char, translated by Nancy Naomi Carlson
Severance Songs (poems), Joshua Corey
Atlas Hour (poems), Carol Ann Davis
New Cathay: Contemporary Chinese Poetry, edited by Ming Di
Sanderlings (poems), Geri Doran
The Flight Cage (poems), Rebecca Dunham
The Posthumous Affair (novel), James Friel
Nothing Can Make Me Do This (novel), David Huddle
Meridian (poems), Kathleen Jesme
Darktown Follies (poems), Amaud Jamaul Johnson
Dancing in Odessa (poems), Ilya Kaminsky
A God in the House: Poets Talk About Faith (interviews),
    edited by Ilya Kaminsky and Katherine Towler
Manoleria (poems), Daniel Khalastchi
domina Un/blued (poems), Ruth Ellen Kocher
Phyla of Joy (poems), Karen An-hwei Lee
Boat (poems), Christopher Merrill
Body Thesaurus (poems), Jennifer Militello
Mary & the Giant Mechanism (poems), Mary Molinary
After Urgency (poems), Rusty Morrison
Lucky Fish (poems), Aimee Nezhukumatathil
Long Division (poems), Alan Michael Parker
Ex-Voto (poems), Adélia Prado, translated by Ellen Doré Watson
Intimate: An American Family Photo Album (memoir), Paisley Rekdal
Thrill-Bent (novel), Jan Richman
Calendars of Fire (poems), Lee Sharkey
Cream of Kohlrabi: Stories, Floyd Skloot
Babel's Moon (poems), Brandon Som
The Perfect Life (lyric essays), Peter Stitt
Swallowing the Sea (essays), Lee Upton
Butch Geography (poems), Stacey Waite
Archicembalo (poems), G. C. Waldrep
Dogged Hearts (poems), Ellen Doré Watson

See our complete backlist at
www.tupelopress.org